Lots of
Grandparents

Lots of
Grandparents

by Shelley Rotner and Sheila Kelly, Ed.D.

Photographs by Shelley Rotner

MILLBROOK PRESS • MINNEAPOLIS

Grandmothers, Grandfathers;
Nanas, Papas;
Memes, Pepes;
Bathis, Jajus;

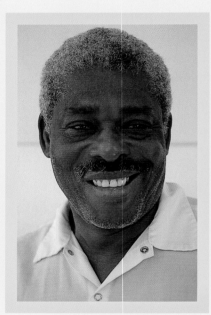

Abuelos, Abuelas;
Gukas, Shoshos;
Poppys, Babas.

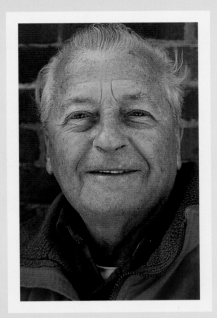

There are lots of grandparents and even great-grandparents.

Sometimes they come to visit,

or you visit them.

Sometimes grandparents
take care of you.

They tell you stories,
share their treasures . . .

and give you presents and treats.

They like to play with you . . .

. . . and are proud of what you can do.

Some grandparents look old and have wrinkles; some don't.

Some move very slowly; some don't.

Some don't see very well.
Some don't hear very well.

Some can't walk very well.
And some have trouble breathing.

Sometimes they live where there are people to take care of them.

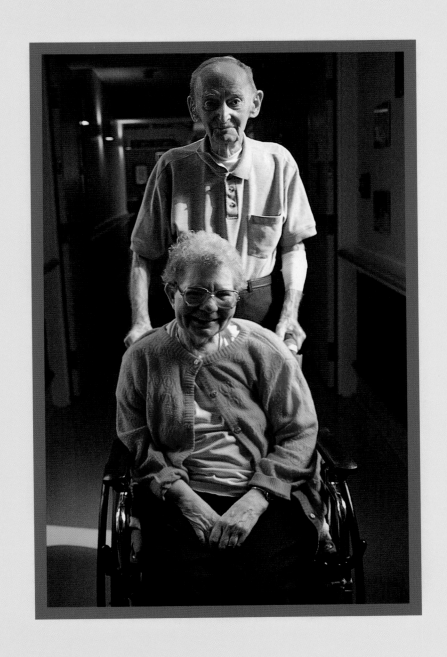

They have friends there and help
each other when they can.

Some grandparents go to work.

Some work at home.

They like to be busy.

And they like to have fun!

Best of all, grandparents love their grandchildren.

It's good there are lots of grandparents!

*In loving memory of
my grandmother. —SR*

*For Ella Kelly, our great Gan,
and all her friends at Upper Canada Lodge
Niagra-on-the-Lake. —SK*

We're grateful to the grandparents and their grandchildren who helped create this book.

Millbrook Press
A division of Lerner Publishing Group
241 First Avenue North
Minneapolis, Minnesota 55401 U.S.A.
Website address: www.lernerbooks.com

Library of Congress Cataloging-in-Publication Data

Rotner, Shelley
Lots of grandparents/Shelley Rotner and Sheila Kelly; photographs
by Shelley Rotner.
p. cm.
ISBN-13: 978-0-7613-2313-6 (lib. bdg. : alk. paper)
ISBN-10: 0-7613-2313-9 (lib. bdg. : alk. paper)
ISBN-13: 978-0-7613-1896-5 (pbk. : alk. paper)
ISBN-10: 0-7613-1896-8 (pbk. : alk. paper)
1. Grandparents—Juvenile literature. 2. Grandparent and
child—Juvenile literature. [1. Grandparents.] I. Kelly, Sheila M. II.
Title.
HQ759.9 .R68 2001
306.874 5—dc21
00-066827

Manufactured in the United States of America
2 3 4 5 6 7 - DP - 10 09 08 07 06 05